THE ART OF MERCY
New and Selected Poems

The acknowledgments appear on page 124 and constitute a continuation of the copyright page.

Cover art: Norman J. Olson, *Still Life with Vase*, Oil on canvas, 2017. With permission of the artist.

Edited by Johnny Cordova
Book design and composition by Dominique Ahkong
Author photo by Mike Buford

ISBN: 978-1-942493-90-7 (paperback)
ISBN: 978-1-942493-91-4 (ebook)

Library of Congress Control Number: 2023939875

Printed and bound in the United States of America
First printing October 2023

HOHM PRESS
P.O. Box 4410
Chino Valley, AZ 86323
(800) 381-2700

hohmpress.com

For all those who have traveled through the dark
without map or flashlight

The Art of Mercy

New and Selected Poems

Robert L. Penick

Beggar Poet Series

Hohm Press

Contents

THE ART OF MERCY

from **EXIT, STAGE LEFT**

from BEWARE THE MADMEN

from BOTTLE OF NIGHT

from BLUE FORMS

WHEN YOU'RE OLD

Author's Note

A lifetime ago I began the obsessive and perhaps life-saving habit of scribbling in school folders, composition books, and whatever legal pad or bit of typewriter paper I could get a hold of. I was fourteen years old and had been grounded for over a year for crimes that were never made clear. My first products were song lyrics and poems that rhymed dreadfully. Even at that primordial stage, I held an implicit belief that the simple act of making simple statements or describing an event would lead me somewhere, a sanctuary or aerie where there would be distance between myself and the sharp edges of the world.

That didn't happen, of course. We carry the world within us, sharp edges and all. But the writing shaped me over the decades, and I in turn shaped the writing, and we each grew into a philosophy that the best and indeed only defense against an irrational, often violent world is to practice kindness and look for beauty in every dark crevice. What I hope these minor poems show is that there is opportunity for goodness and mercy in any situation. The worse the situation, the greater the opportunity.

So be kind. It doesn't usually cost much.

THE ART OF MERCY

Kicking Goals

Eight o'clock on Christmas morning
and you're kicking footballs off a tee.
The grass on the field lies brown and buried
beneath two inches of crusted snow.
The only tracks here are yours, left as you
run forward after every kick
to retrieve the battered, fraying ball.
Everyone has to be good at something,
the adults tell you, and this is all
you can think of. School is a puzzle
where the solution keeps changing.

You'll be thirteen in seven weeks
and you don't think much about girls,
just who you are in this world and
how you can justify your existence.
Twenty months until high school.
Maybe you'll make junior varsity.
Wear the jersey, show your parents.
Maybe you'll go to college, turn pro.
You place the ball on the tee, step back,
imagine it sailing straight through
the future's fanged, open mouth.

Dexterity

We are the damaged ones
making the art
singing the songs
acting the roles
to distract you
from self, time
and mortality.
You can find us
at three a.m.
on the public radio
cleaving time
planting hope,
meaning, joy and,
perhaps, stamina.
We wait your tables
serve your coffee
stock your shelves
then work our quiet
unhinged hours
to create the things
that keep you
human.

10

Here is your perfect moment:
Eating lunch on the bank of
the Ohio River. Rolled oysters,
twist of lemon, with diet soda
off to the side.
It's fifty-eight degrees,
overcast, the wind tousling
the napkins. Your hoodie is up
to protect your ears and pate.

Above you hangs an Edvard Munch sky.

When we said, 'your perfect moment,'
we didn't mean *perfect* perfect,
like a dream date with a gymnast
or a vacation in Elysium,
but the best you will get
in this incarnation.
The hair isn't growing back
and the scars won't wash off.
Every moment is bartered.

So enjoy this early March,
with its breeze that chills
but does not freeze head and heart.
There are days coming, both
warmer and colder, like a snake
following its own tail.

Selling Bibles

The first door is the most difficult.
Every single day it is.
Always the peeling paint and
a howling television
behind that wall of No.

Rap your frost-chilled knuckles
against the plywood and wait
the long December wait.
Your shoes are duct-taped and
dirty, each a hybrid box

held together by hope.
The TV volume cuts down
and you know you're at bat.
Take that breath, widen those eyes.
It's the morning's first audition.

The door finally opens to show
a woman's face, blanched and tired,
wanting nothing from anyone
except relief and rest
and a month's worth of hope.

But you're a child selling bibles.
The woman can't resent your knock,
your shoes, your dirty face. She says,
"No, thank you" but, behind that door,
she offers you a prayer.

Twelve Years Old

All of a sudden we were feigning God,
with broken windows and mysterious fires.
We came alive within a blanket of sweat,
a surge of a hormone we could not name.

The disease was hyperactivity
and we fought it with exhaustion, movement,
with desperate thoughts of girls serious
about the art we knew little of.

Poem of Fright

The world is full of monsters
and some of them are us.
For every behemoth lurking
in the night there are seven
burrowed deep within
the anthills of our psyche.

A terrible place, the mind,
with its dark passageways
and hidden corridors.
Each room might offer up
its own ogre, a new version
of our darkest self.

Lvov, Poland, March 1943

Long before it was necessary to hide
in the primitive labyrinth
beneath the city, Ignacy Chiger
built a fake wall to hide his
children. Unscarred and showing
its newness, it was detected.
The family was dragged out, the
youngest crying. Ignacy bought them
from Janowska's gates with tears,
a gashed skull and his wristwatch.
The cyanide vials his wife clutched,
white bones showing beneath Semitic skin,
could be saved for another time.
That evening she listened as other wives,
now childless, hurled themselves
from rooftops, each landing
with a sound more terrible
than grief.

4-21-93

One day while walking
in the rain
I noticed all
my time
slipping
past me. I decided
not to lose one
more moment by
doing detestable
things
like nothing, or
worrying, or daydreaming
and instead concentrate on
the important matters of
living, breathing, and
this simple way of
praying with the eyes.
Everyone who knew
me then now thinks
I'm crazy, but it
takes courage to
go crazy, to lose
all one has and
summon happiness.
I live secure in
my illness, arms
outstretched, my
crippled spirit
finally touching
clouds.

Trailer Park, Valdosta, Georgia, 1983

With the windows open you can hear
the whisper of the traffic on I-75
telling you there's a world
occurring elsewhere.

You console yourself with television,
fortified wine, occasional 8-ball
at a tavern a mile away.

Days at the chair factory
make you glad to get home
until the cars on I-75
get into your ear, like the voice
of a lover on the telephone,
saying, *"I don't know you, Honey,
but please, please come on home."*

Safe

There are no words here
inside your slender arms. No ideas.
No discussion of aesthetic
virtue, no ideal of pleasure
to be counted off and surveyed
like an acre of fallow land.
There are no requirements here.
No accidents, no plans.
Quantity is without number
and lacking does not exist.
What remains is stillness, silence,
and your heart's delicate music.

Foster Child

If you have to invite yourself every year,
Thanksgiving dinner alone is better,
less lonely than listening to former siblings,
playmates, blanket hogs interact with their
children, their real kin, the bond there
bulletproof to government subsidies and
court injunctions.

You are a neglected appendage they need
to gnaw from their bodies. You mattered,
once, were as necessary as a sloth's tail,
to help with homework, fold up laundry.
Being the oldest, you mowed the lawn
and protected them from predators.
Now a blood relation needs your space at the fire.

Culling

The sunflower stalks lie in the backyard
like carnage, like old beliefs.
Syrup oozes from the rotten blossoms.
Longer than a man, they waste in the
sunlight, they atrophy, they burn.

Above them, the gnats hover. Each drawn to
the sugar of death, sucking vitality
from the sweetness of the flowers' failure.
They feast on cellulose, banqueting
on what the sparrows and jaybirds disdain.

What is left of these stalks will be shredded
and spread upon November ground. Time feeds
on itself the way next year's sunflowers
will gather strength from these. The way
darkness births twilight, and twilight, dawn.

First Snow

And the winter arrives like a rude in-law:
Unannounced, in the night, making a mess of
everything you've planned for days.

You wanted to walk the trails, watch the final
spent leaves surrender to time and gravity,
falling like words in an empty room.

But now the paths are muddy with the snow's thaw,
and the leaves are sealed with dripping ice, making
this setting best viewed from the car.

So, humor that ill-bred relative, the one
whose wet galoshes seep into your carpet.
Start the car, drive, show them the sights.

Odd People with Little Dogs

They come to the park with their mutts,
their hounds, their pedigreed Pekingese
to walk the same paths, sniff the same
shrubbery, investigate the perfume
of mysterious strangers, as they had
the previous week, or three days ago,
or at this exact time yesterday.

These folk are rumpled, disheveled,
as disorganized as Bowery bums
shuffling along at midnight.
Their animals are better kept:
Expensive sweaters and, sometimes, boots
to keep the cold out and the mud off.
They are dandies, with chauffeur and valet.

They each have the other.
What one needs, the other possesses:
The fawning look, the belly rub, gestures
and counter-gestures. They are as bonded
and interdependent as a spoke
in the wheel that circles their days.

Bath Day

Clean for the first time in a month,
the dogs run laps around the dining room,
figure 8's through the den.
They bound up to me, euphoric,
to have their collars put back on.

Noodles, the ancient back-alley found poodle,
when I scratch his wet, swayed back,
cranes his head at the ceiling and grins,
his eyes showing the completeness
I've searched for all my life.

No Postscript

At three a.m. she wakes and,
thinking it's almost morning,
pads quietly to the shower.
Once immersed in the warm torrent,
she lathers her flesh. Passes
the bar of soap lightly over
the tattooed orchid she got
when the two of you drove
twelve hours to Key West simply
to watch the sun set.
Once rinsed, she snaps the faucets
shut with a mindless efficiency.
Towels off. Steps lightly
into the kitchen, wrapped in her
burgundy robe, to make coffee.
When she notices the time
she laughs and taps herself lightly
on the forehead. Draping her
robe on a chair, she crawls back
into bed. Shivering slightly,
she lets sleep retake her.
Never once thinking
of you.

Going Wrong

At first the changes are subtle;
her hand does not instinctively
grasp at yours during those
afternoon walks through the park.
Expressions of endearment
are milder and less frequent
and "I love you, too" becomes
a jerk of the knee.
Even the sex has lost its
feeling of newness, not yet
mechanical, but routine.
Each bite lacks the magic sting.
Finally you're the loser
in a popularity contest
with the television.
You do what you can—
cope, not beg—
and cherish what is left.
Rub her back while she
watches *Masterpiece Theatre*,
make friends with her cat.

Seeds

This is how it begins.
At dinner she talks too long
about the new man at work,
then catches herself,
changes the subject.
Asks you about the flavor
of your tofu.
Her eyes drift across
the restaurant when you
mention the house she wanted
you to buy, as if
needing a face to
grab onto that
isn't yours.

Cleaning

I'm dropping empty cat food cans
into the recycling bin.
There have been a dozen of them
sitting on the kitchen counter
for weeks. The house stinks of them.
I take the garbage outside,
remove your clothes from the dryer,
fold them up and put them on
the dresser. When I wash the dishes
I handle each piece gingerly,
trying not to wake you.
Later I will fill up a basket
with the dirty clothes I find
on the floor. This is not my house
and you are an adult.
We are becoming something other
than lovers.

Trace

You're not going to haunt my house.
I have too many ghosts here already.
There's the emaciated woman
who would drink until my beer was gone,
get angry and storm out.
The straw man who recited
from memory poems he devised
in prison. The mad wife who, I swear,
could throw a shoe around a corner.
The dog that ran out on moving day
straight beneath the wheel of a Ford.
Then all the boarders:
The pale girl in junior high
who moved away after kissing me.
The dead daughter who never goes out.
So many personalities
walking those corridors.
I don't know where you'd sleep.

Change

You keep having the same dream:
You are home from a long journey,
a new suit on your back.
Opening your suitcase, you unpack.
The clothes are all too small for you.
Much too small, like those of a dwarf.
You wore them, danced in them,
had your picture taken in those rags
at several points during your trek.
But now they are washcloths,
handkerchiefs, dress-up clothes
for children's dolls.
You fold them. Set them aside.

Your Future, Burning

It is the sixth of July and fireworks
are Buy One Get Two Free at the stand
in the Dollar General parking lot.
Ninety-six degrees Fahrenheit
and the cars crawl, armored ants,
to their destinations. Movement
and purpose. For one hundred years
society has had a lit fuse attached
to its overfed, all-consuming ass.
Now the buffets are failing,
mankind's muscle atrophying
into a gelatinous mass of
sloth and privilege. Turn up
the air conditioning, venture out
only at dawn and dusk, and pay
no attention to the acrid scent
of this world on fire.

Penultimate

There's hardly anything left of them,
the tottering loners who visit
the supermarkets and public libraries,
moving cautiously, surveying the terrain
like experienced soldiers crossing
unfamiliar territory.

They know these spaces by heart, though,
the circuit through the pharmacy,
the path to the corner table at
the coffee shop, where they can observe
the world through a dusty window.

Still, they move with care, knowing
the soil beneath their feet is shifting
a perceptible amount each day
and will continue to drift until they
catch up with those they've outlasted.

The Gentleman

For Gilbert Michael Smith, d. 2010

He walks by my house every day,
makes his purchase at the liquor store
and returns, carrying a small package
under one arm.
Something is very wrong with the other;
there are no bones in it, anywhere.
It hangs from his shoulder like a flaccid
balloon. When the wind blows, his fingers
flutter like confetti and his forearm bends
at impossible angles.

I talked to him once, walking back,
each of us with our bag of mercy.
He was a kind man, polite, intelligent,
without anyone, waiting to die.
A great sadness hung over him.

I've never seen him speak to anyone else.

One day he will stop walking to the liquor store
and no one will notice but me.

Four A.M., Radio On

Four A.M., radio on.
I'm dreaming of my sweetheart
at home in bed with her husband
sleeping through the storms
passing through my head.
I think, "How convenient
an arrangement we have,
that she has the daylight
with me, then escapes
back into normalcy
just as the sun sets."
Woody Chancy, the
midnight Roadhouse deejay
plays, "Don't Worry, I'm Comin'"
and, beneath me, I feel
the earth turning and
the dawn racing like madness
to catch me.

Photograph of My Father on My Second Wedding Day

He is standing in the doorway
smiling like he's at the circus.
He is wearing his only suit.

Behind him, Brian Wilson eats
deviled eggs without any hands.
His audience is applauding.

If I had known getting married
would bring my old man so much joy,
would light his eyes up like neon,

I would have wed with every
knock-kneed brillo-haired enchantress
that managed to crawl down my street.

It was always that way: Trying
to make that small connection
and mastering the trick too late.

Drowning

When the last bubble of carbon dioxide
escapes your lips, watch it rise.
It contains your childhood, and the childhood
of your grandparents, and the shape of your
father's hand in the womb. A Kentucky
farmhouse and, even now, the toil
of your family's slaves.

It will ascend through the murk
toward a light that is greater than you,
that holds a power you once thought yours.
Reach for them, both the light and the
rising orb. Pay one last gesture
to both of your mutual realms.

Duty

He was sixty-three years old
before he got it right, before
he left off missing being missed
or loved or wanted, and got on with
the rituals that would become
his life. Days moved like a carousel,
each dawn that bright yellow horse
passing by again.

This is what you have left
the walls told him, and he took
the hours and joined them together
until he had something to show
that damned bright steed.

And so he remains,
punctual to his habits and mission
until his heart and the sun
burn themselves out.

You Already Know

Pour one out for Sisyphus,
that eternally suffering dope.
He's still pushing his stone,
you know, up that cruel hill and
blaming it on some blonde handful
of desire and indiscretion.
It never ends, you know,
eternity spools out so far
you never get a glimpse
of the end, or near the end
or even the Goddamned middle.
And it is *his* stone, you know,
bought and financed on behalf of
his misunderstood concepts of
power and consequence.
He's paying for it right now
bolting on body panels
at the Ford plant, or
punching out license plates
in some penitentiary.
Desk or farm or shop floor,
if you cut him loose, he would
only ensnare himself again.
Dogs on leashes have better
judgment and self-preservation.
This son of a bitch
will never learn.

New

I want to be brave
at New Year's, at
just-before-dawn
or in the waiting room
of my oncologist.

I want to smile
before I take
the examination,
exhale before jumping
from Helios.

There is such a place
as serenity
and I want to forward
my mail there,
pack a tiny bag

then float that way
on a stone boat,
leaving grief and
that monster Samsara
behind.

Distancing

When I see you at work now
I don't want to throw arms
around your frail shoulders.
I don't want to run my hand
through your tinted hair.
You now share space
with ex-wives, second cousins
and people I sort of knew
in high school. Still,
I can remember lying
beneath your sheets, your body
snug against me as you slept,
my hands touching the one thing
in life I could believe.

What We Had As Love

I stroke your back with my hand as we awake.
Notice the fever of your hangover.

"Stay still, baby. I'll get some water and aspirin."
Making you drink the whole glassful.
Sometimes you vomit, and I hold your hair
as you cough up the remnants of last night's wine.

I watch you apply your makeup before
you waitress the lunch crowd.

Closing the door, hearing your car start.
I open a beer. Empty the ash trays.

Embrace the prodigal day.

Finished Poem

I wish I had the strength
to reach down and pull you up
with me. I would show you
this view from ground level,
where the boots are not
so tall, where the clouds
are not so high, where today
is a morning green with life.

I wish I had the knowledge
to show you what I gather
from the cars on the street
and the laughter behind closed windows.
But I do not know what I feel,
I only feel it. That a great and
giving promise lurks the shadows,
even as we search for light.

Something New

It's very difficult
loving someone
who's not tragic
or destructive
or fatally flawed.
The hours don't have
that emptiness
you can crawl inside.

When it rains
it is just rain.
Not something
wrapping its arms
around you
like a perfectly
sad goodbye.

Procession

What was it, shining so brightly in their hands?
Perhaps passion? Perhaps hope?
Perhaps it was different for each soul;
one a Crucifix, another a cudgel,
a third with a bouquet of fire.
Yet another carried a snifter of kindness
and one more a bottle of night.

They flowed in an unbroken line
topping the hill to the East then
crossing the plains to disappear
past the purple hills in the West.
Some were cheerful, full of mirth.
Some wore tragic masks.
Some very few were penitent.

Thus they made their passage,
each with their own separate light.

All that I have done

in this life has been an attempt
to gild every rusted bottle cap,
every broken window,
every bent, useless swing set
in every backyard, with glitter,
with stardust, with the magic
that children know when they
watch an airplane pass over
and have the impossible proven.

I have built a great castle
only to find the wiring faulty,
a draft in the bedrooms
and the floors uneven.

This view from the rampart,
though, of the sun setting
on the churches and the bars
and the brokerage houses
cannot be equaled by
any offering from
an ordinary life.

Coffeehaus Poem #487

He sits in coffee shops and fast-food joints,
occasionally weepy-eyed, staring out windows
and scratching into a school notebook.
This part isn't important, is less than
exponents of nothing repeated
to the end of the block and back.

Life comes with an owner's manual,
but it's to a different model.
In fact, a different brand entirely.
Knowing this, he compensates, watches
YouTube tutorials:
How to build a world.

His mailbox fills up with offers of
cash back, burial insurance, systems
to keep his home and vehicle safe from
unwanted entry. He has too much safety,
he knows, and it has cost him more than
the replacement value of this scarred life.

The Last Ones

They seemed easier to spot thirty years ago,
or perhaps my eye was keener.
The freaks, the misfits, true artists
who wagered their entire lives on
finding the perfect ending to a poem,
or a melody that would break hearts
for a hundred years.

These people stood out like chancres
on the flesh of blind, blinking society.
Their dress and manners signaled fires:
We are different: We breathe different air,
exchange foreign coin. We are sedition.
They strayed from the herd and
set their course from novel stars.

Now the world is redivided between
the angry and the scared, no room
at the margins for painters adding gilt
to a picture so tightly framed.
Still, at bus stops and in supermarkets,
perhaps at the DMV, you'll see a secret
sculptor or finagler of verse.

Personals

I'd like to find some desiccated
shell of a woman, tired of failure and
full of nervous tics, always pushing
her hands out into the dark, beyond
the candlelight and television glow,
reaching into the abyss of night
to rummage for her meaning.

Let her be a whore, a former fool
or someone who bet on the wrong man
and lost, badly, wearing the scars,
tracks, and crow's feet as proof that life
can be an endless stream of rejection slips
from parents, lovers, schools, banks,
employers, and God.

Let us find one another and step
quietly into shadows of our own
devising; let us grow mad
with genius, fat with promise, and
let us carve ourselves into this world
like brilliant, beautiful wounds.

A Fine Thread

A message for the horse-faced boys and girls
who will never know love,
pear-shaped, with pig eyes
and dandruff dusting their shoulders
like they are figures in snow globes,
existing apart from the world,
no oxygen, no warmth,
and only intermittent light:

There is a fine thread within you all
that no one has managed to cut
or knot or pull loose from you
and that is your beauty, your grace,
and your symmetry. Hold them out,
both hands, palms upward and open.
See the great gift you've been hiding
in each clenched fist.

The Ghost of Tammy Thompson

edges down 4th Street, dragging
her pitted, bent aluminum walker
alongside her. Her feet scuffle
against the pavement
and everything else.
With a reptile's precision
she inches across great swaths
of uneven asphalt, grim consequence,
never realizing what brought her
to this state, to this tired town,
to this slow march of rust.

Sewing a Button

You've not done this before,
stopping time to repair
a past accident, twenty
minutes spent trying to
thread the needle before
googling the words
How to thread a needle.
You've found most great projects
have a facilitator, something to
string a route through the rapids,
and you find the needle threader
in the army surplus kit,
make an off-center knot
in the line and single-thread
the past back into place.

Remembering the Dead

Raining, again.
It's a sweet flood and
I slept through it
thirteen hours today.
Woke up.
The world had turned
and I thought of you
crusted, frozen in the past
like an ancient mosaic.
In the kitchen
on bare feet
I can make excuses,
microwave the newspaper.
Boil green tea.

Mid-November

This is the time of year
when life seems most natural.
Leaves falling, a cold breeze
beneath the front door.
Time to burrow deep, put
plastic over the windows,
caulk into every crevice.
Make the old house impenetrable
to winds that might bring harm.

No sense in stopping there.
Turn off the answering machine
or, better still, unplug the phone.
Ignore the insistent rapping
at the defective front door.
Let the mail pile high, unread,
while the dime store radio
plays Tchaikovsky and you sit,
nearly warm.

Just Checking

Into those ambiguous days
between Christmas and New Year's
you crept, like a virus
or anniversary.

Years ago I left you behind,
all green eyes and golden legs,
on a pyre of consequence
and failure.

You are still gone, and
I appreciate that, a small gift
we exchange each day, like
a plate of ashes or chalice of fog.

The Art of Mercy

begins with surrender.

Forget about celestial repayment
of dollars bestowed on beggars.
Forget about your fortune's wheel
spinning upward each time
you let an elderly driver
pull into traffic.

That rain-drenched hitchhiker
you drove two counties
past your destination?
You'll get nothing in return.

The five dollar bill
you gave the busker
in Central Park?
It was only a gift.

Let go of your notions
of compensation, karma,
and compassion.
You don't just take
the hitchhiker down the road.
He takes you as well.

Master this and discover
Charity. Grace. Love.

Purchase

I knew I'd need a cane someday
so I examined one
at the Catholic thrift store.
Admired its heft and
sturdiness. You could go off
to war leaning on a cane
like that, you could
circumnavigate the earth
with that lumber in hand.
It was pitted, marked with
scars and dings, the former
owner now dead,
I realized.
I put it back
among the old radios
and knick-knacks,
walked outside, surveyed
the blue sky.
Then walked back in,
made my investment
in the future.

Winter Zen

The furnace is a mindfulness bell
and I am an unworthy but earnest monk.
That quiet *click* on January's coldest night
returns me to the core, returns me
to gratitude for warm air about my body,
warm tile beneath my bare feet.
The simple knowledge of food in the cupboard,
fire in the furnace, the rent paid
through the month of July.

If few people love me, that is okay,
and if they seldom show their affection, fine.
I have the *click* of the thermostat
and the rush of heat through the vents
to bring me back to the circle
of breathing, thinking, remembering,
This art of always returning.

from EXIT, STAGE LEFT

Slipstream Press, 2018

Winner of the 2018 Slipstream Chapbook Contest

You Cannot Say These Things Were Not Done for You

Your parents' upstairs tenant, Rucker,
a half-baked, half-broken factory man,
would take you to the Uptown Theatre
and talk you into R-rated matinees.

He only looks like he's twelve.
I should know. I'm his Dad.
Been feedin' him all these years
but he don't grow any.

After the movie, he'd park in front
of the Sen Den dance club,
leaving you in the car, but
sending out a barely clad stripper
to deliver you a soda.

With eyes agog you'd thank the lady,
who was Pegasus and Siren combined,
then tamp the ice with the straw.
Turning the key in the ignition,
you listened to the Beatles on WKLO.

1974. You were ten years old.
The world was an unbuttoned blouse.

Exit, Stage Left

My mad sprint across so many calendars
will end one day. Likely I will see it
coming from kilometers away:
The fall to the worn carpet,
ragged breathing,
staring at a fixed point until
it collapses like a star and disappears.

I will go out with a schoolboy's smirk
upon my face, knowing the birds
will chirp and carry on each spring
and the great wheel of pain
will roll on without my frail shoulder
guiding it. Hearts will beat
bright as cardinals while
big monster life stamps in circles
and I lie vacant
in my grave.

The First Time He Saw Her Naked

He felt like an unworthy explorer
on the shore of a new continent.
The first things he noticed were
the delicate slope of her shoulders,
the falling contour of her breasts,
the slight swell of her stomach.
He wanted to pinch the flesh
between her hip and ribcage
to see if the earth trembled.
She was gawky; bones sticking out
where the map said hollows,
arms thinner than initial surveys
indicated. A wild land.

Then he was into the country.
A strange, tangled world
with magnificent rivers flowing
back to a shore he'd already
forgotten.

Recovery

"God doesn't plant in straight rows."
– Matthew Haughton

You show up at the door,
full of opiate and promise,
hold your brand-new heart out
like a broken oyster shell and
tell me about your thirty days
of sobriety.

I know you're lying, can see
it in the dilated pupils,
the hopeful, empty smile,
your hands busy weaving
the story you tell.
It's okay. I love you.
We're all doing the best we can.

Lord knows there's nothing else
left to do.

What to Do When the Night is Done with You

Pick up the guitar from its place in the corner,
knock it back into tune.

Wipe the kitchen counters clean of regret,
then make sure the tortoise has water.

Straighten every photograph on the walls
while not looking anyone in the eye.

Catalogue every day of your existence,
then count each new passing moment.

There are always fields to be mown,
even on this moonless night.

Reminder

This is the 17th of October.
Not on the calendar, but for you.
You've flown through fifty years
of cheap beer, fellatio from
hausfraus, DUIs with no fatalities,
and no woman who ever said
"I love you" and meant it
for very long.

Tonight, the radio plays something soft,
a sonata to massage your soul.
You sift the mail, find it all sand.
Not even the chip of a diamond
here on your private beach.
Another week has passed since you last
surveyed your animus and ambition
only to find both lacking.

This is the 17th of October
and the leaves fall now like the scales
from your eyes. You struggle to focus,
like a 19th century photographer trying
to catch Pegasus above the ground,
snapping a thousand shutters closed,
finally getting it right
in the very last frame.

Note: The last stanza refers to Eadweard Muybridge, 1830-1904

Retirement

You're 65 years old and you are sitting in your backyard,
drinking light beer and listening to Brahms on the radio.
The wind makes the Japonica bush and your
remaining hair dance like seaweed in a riptide.

They took everything from you at the factory:
Hair, teeth, testosterone.
They took nearly everything.

The sky isn't as impossibly blue
as it was 50 years ago, but it will do.
Geese honk overhead, heading back north.

The sun makes you feel like
a successful clay pot.

The End of June

The old man at the corner bus stop—
there without fail each morning at eight—
disappeared either two weeks or six months ago.
I'm not sure which.

Was 1987 the year I dated the girl
with the long auburn hair?
Perhaps it was 1986.
I was at the university, I know.
I remember the mole on her back
but not her birthday or eye color.

Things move away more quickly now
and fewer things take their place.
I walk around this city, peering
into faces empty and bloated
like drowning victims.

Last night I saw a bird fall
from a wire, wings unmoving
before it hit the street.

History

Listen for it, Myrra.
Listen really hard.
It sounds like ice cubes
falling into an empty glass
on the other side of the pool.
It sounds like sand blowing
100 meters down the beach.
It makes the noise
of tattoo ink fading
over the course
of thirty years.
You can hear it
in your popping ankles
and in the puddles
after a storm.
It was always there
like tinnitus or
the refrigerator's hum.

We never notice the Sirens
until the chorus stops.

And what does it all mean?
Not a Goddamned thing.

Franklinton, North Carolina, 1969

You must write all this down
before you forget.

The Askews' gas station and grocery store
across the railroad tracks and down
a path lined with red-rusted bedsprings
and the corpses of stoves and ice boxes.

The baby rabbit that one fine dog
held squirming in his jaws as you
chased them down the trail hollering
"Let it go, let it go."

The Askews' had Mobil gasoline
for 31cents a gallon
and candy for two to five cents.
Pixie Stix, pure sugar, a nickel a rush.

It was a 45-minute walk down the tracks
to Franklinton. Three miles.
Uncle Clifton lost his legs climbing a freight
trying to beat that time.

That accident was before you were born, though.

Long before you mattered,
if you ever mattered at all.

Boneyard

The tombstones cling to the hillside
like raindrops to a window.
At any moment they might tumble
end over timely end
down to the road.

A bird pecks at the moss of one
and finds enough insects to live
an hour, a day, a week.

Meanwhile Eternity waits beneath the grass,
sleepy and heavy-lidded,
quiet as a cloud.

4th of July, 2008

There is a termite gnawing steadily
through a beam in your cellar.
There is a cancer cell nesting,
hungry, in your marrow.

They are the beginning of things
that will transform your world
from hollow to full,
from grey to blood red,
from distant to painfully
immediate.

They are a burden and a curse
but so is monotony
and who can say which bundles
of protein, fiber, and need
matter most
in the complexity
of this earth?

Photograph of Rucker Kelly Sitting on the Front Porch

That's my life, too:
Trying to look presentable
after toiling in a
factory of stink.
Looking hopeful
in my mid-forties.

We both tried hard,
you and I,
at the wheel, the plow,
the packing house and
house of correction.

And we worked
like the desperate,
and we loved
like slaves until
our defective hearts
overtook us.

We were not survived.

What Got Him

Nothing.

That's what
got him
in the end.
Not the stress
of bills or
the ache of love
unreciprocated.
Not a bolt of
lightning nor the
unrelenting
march of time.

What got him
was a lacking,
a space of air
where something
should have been.

Like a shelf,
meant to hold
great books,
standing
empty.

from BEWARE THE MADMEN

Chapbook from Another Mule Press, 2005

Getting Sober Again

This is how it must be started:
Microwaved tea at three A.M.,
a two-mile walk at four.
Not killing the paperboy when
the morning edition lands short.
You shower early, breakfast early,
leave for work fifteen minutes prematurely.
To hurry is to stir your nerves
into a troubling stew. Uh-uh.
You step slowly, stopping often
to survey the landscape, adjust for
road construction and city buses.
Above all, you keep moving, never
turning to see what monster
is stepping into your footprints,
laying his breath upon your back.

Learning to Count to One

Propped up on an elbow trying to count
the faint freckles scattered like wishes
beneath your eyes, across your nose,
I notice for the first time the single
chicken pock mark floating above your brow.

Beneath my finger that cavity of
distant illness and forgotten loss
hums like a brave whisper.

The street outside is quiet with
the dawn barely broken.

You go on sleeping and I touch you,
search, catalog each wound.

Keeping Things New

is harder than it sounds,
making each moment crack
like ice under heavy boots.
One must be inventive,
even diabolical,
with the glance, the caress,
the testament of longing
whispered at midnight.
One must work at
the spontaneity,
devise games for the mouth,
hiding places for
every finger.
One must learn new ways
of being quiet.
Without discovery, love becomes
a hamburger from a drive-thru.
A car you've had for years
that never runs right.
A bad haircut or
her least favorite flowers.

Map Making

Every man must be a cartographer,
making a resolved schema
of all his wanderings, surveys,
mad expeditions and
luckless forays into
the tangled wilderness.
Each highway must be cataloged,
every footpath, side street
and mountain pass detailed.
Much of this countryside
can only be seen at night,
its valleys and ridges
barely discernible
beneath a clouded moon.
Knowing this landscape
is important, lest the traveler
fall asleep at the reins,
waking much later
to find himself lost.

Beware the Madman

The one in the dirty gray house
seven doors from the liquor store.

The one whose windows are dark
on Halloween.

The one who talks to stray dogs
and dead lovers.

If you offer conversation
his tongue will knot up
like a necktie.

He does not need help
with his yard. He likes it
tangled, like his thoughts.

When it rains at night
he imagines the earth renewed.

If you hand him a bouquet
he will hear each flower scream.

from **BOTTLE OF NIGHT**

Chapbook from Hemispherical Press, 2004

Writing Desk, Five A.M.

None of the lovers matter now,
none of the lost jobs, the spent cash,
the departed women who forgot you
more quickly than you forgot yourself.
You wear a mask of fatigue and
indifference, skulking away at
your literary endeavors like a termite
taking on a redwood. Single-handedly,
no support group or supply line
behind you, no fan club or even
friends who truly believe in you.
But you keep working on the books,
the poems, the out of tune rhymes.
Hoping one day to see a turn of phrase
or glowing image that vindicates
this monstrous run across
so many calendars.

Late

I used to be a man, here,
somewhere in the folds
of soft flesh and cowardice.
I once stood upright, spine
resilient as a sapling,
mind murky as Texas mud.

It was better that way,
body strong for new jobs,
new burdens, new lovers.
Intellect was not needed
for warm embraces, hods
of concrete, or pitchers
of draft beer.

Tonight I am aged,
skin too enormous for
what remains of desire.
My telephone sits, quiet,
and the walls reach beyond God
as I read bad reviews
and ask why I built this box
to live in.

4: 15 P.M.

This is the part of the day
when I'd like to call my sweetheart
and say, "Hey, honey, I'm so tired
but I got it all done. And I'm waiting
here like ashes for your kind hands
and warm water to fashion me back
into clay, a man. Your fingers are like
God to me, after torment, those
hard points on my flesh."

Then she would knock at my door
and come in with thoughts of January,
saying, "I will tear you into confetti,
then create you anew.
When you are ribbons beneath
the knives of my nails, I will place you
into two piles: That which I love to hold
and that which I covet. The second
to be discarded. The first, treasured."

Crystal

You were the one with the calluses
on your thumb and index finger.
You were the one without shoes.
You carved the names of your children
into your thighs. Let them stand
like cemetery markers.

A failing comet, you fled yourself
and dove into that land
where monsters lie still
and parents are reborn
whole and new.

You wanted weightlessness, release
from the world's gravity.

I see you now,
hanging stars in
an otherwise
barren and
lightless
sky.

The Wine is Always Waiting

The wine is always waiting
When you get tired of fighting
When you get tired of walking upright
When you get tired of trading punches
With opponents who are always behind you.

The wine is always waiting
When you can't take the stupidity
When you can't take the repetition
When you notice the house odds
Are much higher than the payoff.

The wine is always waiting
When even sunlight cuts you
When every breath brings regret
When God sees you, then turns his head
When you pull the nails from your heart.

It sits, patient.

Midnight at the Quarterpole Bar and Lounge

Drunk, stumbling, I walked down
to be with the other humans.
I treasure solitude, but on
this particular night darkness
gnawed at me like cancer.
Halfway there, an older
Hispanic man rolled up on
a bicycle. Asked me where
the nearest tavern might be.
He rode ahead and I met him
at the Quarterpole. We watched
the people dancing, laughing,
carrying on with a
manic desperation.
They were racetrack workers:
Grooms, exercise riders,
hot walkers. All of us poor.
Owners and trainers must drink
across town, I told my friend.
His name was Gregorio. Said
his boss couldn't win a race
if he stabled Secretariat.
Just before last call he leaned
into me and whispered,
"Everyone here is missing a
piece of something. The sad ones
laugh too much, unhappy lovers
cling like skin to bone.
The poorest players buy
the most rounds.
Everyone hides a secret.
What is yours, my friend?"

Memorial Day

It's been awhile since I've felt the gravel
of the emergency lane beneath my feet,
waited for some highway-borne Samaritan
to deliver me a good distance down the road
to a place far away from
wherever I happened to be.
I was hungry for America then,
to know every inch of her,
every scar, crease, and pimple,
the way a man hungers
for his favorite lover.
Now, years later, I have seen the strip malls
of San Pedro, the franchised coffee shops
of San Francisco and New York and the two
remaining department stores left in this country.
The buildings are everywhere,
like monuments or citadels.
There is no purpose in exploring
this country any longer.
Every city is the same lover.

Error

The mistake is
thinking your bones
are more special
than other bones
that your blood
is more blessed
or unique
that your heart
is purer
than that of, say,
the retired janitor
who waits patiently
at the corner
for a southbound
evening bus.

Woman, Custer, Kentucky, 1999

She tosses her hair behind her,
then offers her face to the sun's imprint.
Leans back against the trunk of a
rusted-red Chevrolet.

Perhaps the sunlight
will preserve them both.

Parking lot of a
franchise gas station.
Fuel and cigarettes,
donuts, coffee, perhaps
air for the tires.

Out back, the sign
on the compressor reads
"Quarters Only."

Inside the station, a man long debates
over the price of wiper blades.

His wife loiters, feels her bones
grow warm, something flowing.
A bonding of light.

I Want You to Tell Me

Why the sun rises
in the same place
every day.

How a foal knows
to arise and walk
an hour after birth.

What the ant thinks
as he carries stones
from his workplace.

Do ants sleep?
If so, do they dream?

I need answers for
these questions.

They gnaw at me
like religious doubt or
the daughter who died
twenty years ago
tonight.

Bottle of Night

Keep it on the tallest shelf
in the darkest corner of any room.
Light is the enemy, for light
holds a cruelty more vulgar than time.

Save it for the sunniest day
when ice cream trucks and children
        rule the streets.
Then you can uncork the vessel
and run slanted into forgiving arms.

Riddle

I am holding a secret in my right hand.
At night, when I do not sleep, I push it
beneath the bed, trapping it between
the mattress and the floor.
The best place for it, usually,
is the back seat of the car, where I can
forget it, leave it, let it age and yellow
in the sun.

Once I mailed it to Madagascar
and it was returned, festooned with
a rainbow of pretty stamps and tape.

Wherever I travel, it arrives
moments before me.
Its mere presence leaves me
bluer than death.

from BLUE FORMS

Chiron Review Press, 1999

Winner of the 1998 Chiron Review Chapbook Contest

Siempre

I remember you touched by holier hands
than mine and leaning into that void of
helplessness, your brown eyes scared with
the realization of who you were not and
what you were not becoming. Your hands
would clutch at any icon: The crucifix,
the phallus, the bottle of mad misery
you poured yourself into, always hoping
for relief wishing for a cure some magic
to change you from poor desperate creature
wash your insides bleach your heart put
back the broken and empty pieces and make
you clean and whole again your hourglass
refilled your high school yearbook face
unlined sixteen years old before everything
went away leaving cold night increased
gravity gut a wet mop inside twisted
wringing wet always slowly unwinding.

I remember you sad and proper reminding yourself
not to beg when the scraps were yours to keep.

8-24-93

...I'm thinking intently now of my own shot soul
and its decline, ten years now of waste and excess
time lost in television and marriages, some
near-miss episodes of unplanned happiness
the quiet murmur of distant dreams
like voices underground.

I'm thinking serenely now of the air
conditioner's hiss and the outside miles away where
flowers are wilted and brown and the aged gasp
for breath they can no longer reach
in this southeastern summer, this
dying of every day.

I'm thinking of a woman I knew
and cool brown bottles of beer the
darkest of St. Louis nighttimes outside
soft music in an expensive hotel room
the light on her hair and the
sheet on her hip.

I am thinking of the moments
past in distraction, the great whirring
of my spirit as it tried to ascend
from the forest of my own worst doubts.
My heart in ruins.
I am thinking now...

13th Poem for America

Time has made midgets of us all—
We grow shorter each generation.
Gone is Odysseus, gone Icarus—
Men who tried great things and, gaming
with their lives, sometimes lost.
Now dwarves furnish the landscape
with mediocrity, vanity,
insignificant victories
over inconsequential foes.

Instead of literature, we page
Reader's Digest. In place of
Thermopylae, colonels lie
to Congress. Wars are fought by
remote control and convenience store
clerks who fend off robbers must find
new work.
It's a sad time we live in, when
giants roam only institutions
and heroes are thought eccentric.

Bigfoot, in that famous film footage,
escaping into the woods—
He may have been the last man.

The Prince

Six P.M.

The Prince of Preston Street pounds down
hot pavement, his thirst unslaked,
toward the shelter of Skip's Bar.
The world stands still.
The moments cleave themselves
before passing. Time gives way
to Ritual, work to something
more essential. An oiling of the
works, a watering of wounds.

Eleven P.M.

The dank night is stinking
like a whore in Sunday Mass.
The Prince of Preston Street, having
exhausted his privilege, wends his
way upstairs to his room above the
inimitable Skip's Bar. His wounds
clean, his sores drained, he traces
sad lines on walls before sleep.

Six-Thirty A.M.

The alarm clock screams. The day
announces itself in short words.
The Prince of Preston Street rolls
from a shortened twin bed and
inspects his sink, offering fragments
of the evening's ritual. He is the
withered remains of the previous night.
He is an archetype and a phoenix.

Retrospect

I jumped from a tree—
I think I was five or six—
and landed on a nail.
It lanced up from
a board. Scrap lumber.
God put it there, I think.
An uncle carried me
into the house. I was
screaming.
My mother soaked the
puncture in
mercurochrome and
said "are you
retarded?"
That was North Carolina
in 1969. Trees and
uncles and terror.
The farm. Stray dogs
and agonies.

The Photograph of Leopold Socha

There was little heroic in your features.
You resembled more of Genet's
babyface than the angular features
of successful men, such as
Wallenberg and Schindler.
Thief, robber, sewer worker.
What chance did you see
in hiding those Jews?
Working in your tunnels you
could have forgotten them,
left them to starvation or
grenades tossed down manholes.

You said it was atonement
that kept you coming back,
risking lamppost gallows,
a firing squad for your family.
But why did you risk taking
the tattered Jewish prayerbook
from the ruins of the ghetto
to give to the poetess?
Why hold the seven-year-old
up to the sewer grate,
promising her she'd see
sunshine and flowers again?

You were a tough little Pole
with only courage to spare.

You remembered your crimes,
but who remembered you?

Through

I am through writing poems
about hearts and souls and love,
the gibberish of lonely fools.

My heart is spoiled meat
and love is as distant from me
as a grade school dance.

I'll write instead of
a woman's breath as
her man enters,

on the workings of her hands
as she closes every window,
catching the air inside.

postcard

I don't know who you are,
this person I'm writing.
In my teens, you were a
phantom, a skinny ghost of
what I would be
when time caught up.

Later, in college, I
smoked a thousand cigarettes,
traced approximations of your
profile, wanted to make you
a hero, put a cleft in your chin
that didn't belong.

Years later, I am still
at that window, razor in
hand, watching my
reflection and the rain.
Each of us wondering
where we first met.

Poem in Memory of My Father

The old man is dead now.
The old man is dead.
And this poem will know no meter.
This poem will read like a stopped watch.
Like last year's calendar.
Like a ticket to Ebbet's Field.
Yellowed, like loss.
This poem will have meaning
like Confederate currency
or a day-old weather forecast.
This poem will roll, then stop
like a flattened tire
or a train without fuel.
This poem will sit like dusty shoes
in a closet.
This poem will have no rhythm
for the music is broken
except for the thought of
a child's voice, somewhere, singing.

The Work

The plumbing is undone
at one end of the house
like my childhood train set
and how the trains
never came back.
My father's tools are scattered
through these rooms and I wonder
how long it would take him
to sort things out.
To couple the pipes and
make the equation.

I have outshone my father
in one vital respect:
I screwed this job up
in half the time
he would have needed
to actually complete it.
Somewhere he is shaking his head
and giving me that ancient look,
the one shot from
fathers to sons
forever.

The Joy of Cofer Avenue

On the stoop outside her apartment
the paper carrier occasionally misfired
and we'd sneak out, furtively returning
with a newspaper. It was a good time,
at the kitchen table with the funnies
while our neighbor stomped outside cursing
William Randolph Hearst. He'd go back in
and we'd carefully refold the sheets and
drop them outside his door.

We thought this was just hilarious
until one day I was outside
trying to get a car to start
and he said, "Hey, I know you've
been reading my paper. It smells like
smoke and the pages are creased up.
But that's okay, you're good kids and
you always put it back."

We never took his paper again.
The thrill was gone for us,
the chase ended. We sat through
our mornings a little older,
sadder, the quiet enveloping us,
some kind of magic locked outside the door.

Small Comforts

I do not think of cardinals
upon rising in the morning
until their summer songs
cut through my malaise.
I often hear them
while brushing my teeth
or pissing
and know that once more
a fragment of beauty
has outlasted night.
And it is small comforts
that move us forward
into the next trench
the next day, the next
task to get through
to simply get through
the next bridge to burn
or engine to stoke
the next weapon
or flower to grasp
with stained, open hands.
It is small comforts
that move me forward—
a pretty girl's smile
across a quiet room, eyes
saying, "I know, and it is not so bad."
Perhaps the morning walk
down the hallway to get the mail
or a midnight call to Tokyo
to talk with angels
in a language better

than my own.
If I've learned one thing, it is this:
Enemies are not worth time
to think of, and kind words
are too precious
to be lost in memory.

It is small comforts
that move us forward.

WHEN YOU'RE OLD

When You're Old (I)

The calendar begins to laugh.
Objects in the rearview mirror
are minuscule compared to
the images you have on file.
Your tattoos have faded to
light gray, like the sky draining
from your eyes.
Why do you persist?

The uncoiling rope fascinates.
Each loop progressively smaller
and offering less, each bight
promising an ending.
Why go on? Pick a reason.
Call it perseverance.
Call it running out the clock.
Call it living in spite.

When You're Old (II)

You begin to forget, and that is
you forgiving yourself for each
hurt you've carried, contraband
smuggled from the past.
It wasn't illegal, but it was wrong,
a sin against yourself
to take those black cutting gifts
and cherish them so long.

With time and distance you begin
to place the wrongs in their graves.
Each unmarked and unhallowed offense
now lies undisturbed.
Each new dawn breaks like
a communion wafer, a bright tarot,
a prayer flag, a signal bell
calling you forward.

When You're Old (III)

You don't let yourself
fall in line anymore.
You don't donate clothes
that are out of fashion
(you wouldn't know fashion
if it approached you with
bows and blinking lights).
You don't get angry
at the rain on Easter
or sad when the wind
reminds you of the past.
You perform simple tasks;
one breath in, one breath out,
never taking eyes off
that silent, ticking clock.

When You're Old (IV)

This world has outgrown us
outpaced and outlasted us
left us in the rearview mirror
waved goodbye with a middle finger
advised us our minutes
will not roll over into
the new data plan and all
previous agreements
have been voided.

This world wants to wish us
the very best in those
pursuits we may find,
what bridges we still
might cross, whatever
hole that offers refuge.

This world thanks us for
participating in
so many revolutions.

When You're Old (V)

You begin sewing the wings
back onto butterflies,
the ones that have not crawled
so far into the past
that grains of pollen are
their only evidence.

You find the survivors
in forgotten places:
On a cassette talk tape
from 1996
or on a city bus
passing in a downpour.

Think of that first girlfriend,
the fat kid in high school
or some other victim
along your warped, staggered
pinball across the years.
Thread needle. Prick thumb. Mend.

Your work is neat, quiet,
a restoration of
flight, grace, and symmetry.
Your hands are not nimble
but you try to repair
every leaf you've torn.

When You're Old (VI)

You swap out the rosary
for a hammerless .38 Special
that fits inside your shirt
like a second heart.

You've known violence,
seen it unfurl like
dinner theater gone wrong
or a mime suddenly
screaming.

It's not pretty, or graceful,
the way it's presented
in movies, all slow motion
and dramatic music.

You move more slowly now,
less sure of yourself, and
you want the best protection
when the music finally
stops.

When You're Old (VII)

You approach happiness
with a benign fury,
carrying out your mission
like a wronged lover,
determined to gain
compensation from a world
that has neglected your worth.

So you take the cruise,
visit the spa. Get every
procedure and injection
that might return
the potential you have spent
on gluttonous dinners
and television reruns.

As the yearbook names fade
from memory, only
to reappear in online
obituary columns,
you crank the heat up and
hope the replacement windows
keep you warm at night.

When You're Old (VIII)

You begin to think
about the way each house
has a soul, a past,
and a memory
of every tread
upon its dusty stairs,
of every child's voice
that has bounced off
its cracked walls.

The kitchens echo
with every breakfast cooked,
every first cigarette smoked
across innumerable
gray mornings.

When you see the ruin
at the end of the road,
with the windows broken
by children nearly grown,
don't believe the legend.

It is not haunted by
recalcitrant spirits.
It is mourning those
who have gone away.

When You're Old (IX)

One day you realize
the cavalry isn't coming
and the vague idea of bliss
that motivated you in youth
did not provide directions
concrete enough to avoid
the wrong turns, did not
account for stalling out and
losing years to the time clock,
the television, the routine.

So you begin to pay attention
to the items that loiter around
your to-do list day after day,
unclaimed baggage and unwon battles.
You visit the park often to sit
by the brook and devise a plan:
First, put your house in order, then
lay claim to this vast, uncertain world.

Acknowledgments

Thank you to the editors of the following publications in which these poems first appeared, sometimes in different forms:

805 Lit Mag: "When You're Old (IV)"
Apple Valley Review: "Purchase"
Bathtub Gin: "Just Checking"
Bluepepper: "The Last Ones"
Bogg: "Bath Day"
Buckle &: "Remembering the Dead"
The Bookends Review: "Winter Zen"
Cedar Hill Review: "Lvov, Poland, March 1943" and "13th Poem for America"
Chiron Review: "You Cannot Say These Things Were Not Done For You," "Writing Desk, Five A.M.," "4:15 P.M," and "Crystal,"
Chrysanthemum 2020 Poetry Anthology: "Your Future, Burning"
Coachella Review: "Dexterity"
Descant: "I Want You to Tell Me"
Free Lunch: "Culling"
Free Verse: "The Art of Mercy"
Fuel: "The Work"
Georgetown Review: "Retirement"
Heeltap: "Twelve Years Old" and "Photograph of my Father on my Second Wedding Day"
Hidden Oak Poetry Journal: "Change" and "Mid-November"
The Higginsville Reader: "Retrospect"
The Hudson Review: "Boneyard"
Kudzu: "No Postscript" and "Drowning"
Joey and the Black Boots: "Riddle"
Licking River Review: "Selling Bibles"
Literary LEO: "History," "Franklinton, North Carolina, 1969," "Photograph of Rucker Kelly Sitting," "Woman, Custer, Kentucky, 1999," "Poem in Memory of my Father," and "When You're Old (V)"
Little Patuxent Review: "Duty"
The Louisville Review: "Learning to Count to One"
Main Street Rag: "Late"
Mas Tequila Review: "Kicking Goals"

The Meadow: "What to do when the Night is Done with You"
Mochila Review: "Poem of Fright" and "Getting Sober Again"
Nerve Cowboy: "Going Wrong," "Seeds," "Trace," "Distancing," "What We had as Love," "Finished Poem," "The First Time He Saw Her Naked," and "The Wine is Always Waiting"
New World Writing Quarterly: "A Fine Thread" and "All that I have done"
Once a City Said: A Louisville Poets Anthology: "Midnight at the Quarterpole Bar and Lounge"
Pearl: "Bottle of Night"
Piker Press: "When You're Old (I)" and "When You're Old (II)"
Pitchfork: "Map Making"
Plainsongs: "The Ghost of Tammy Thompson"
Presa: "Four A.M., Radio On"
Quiddity: "What Got Him"
Rainbow Curve: "Keeping Things New"
The Remembered Arts Journal: "Procession"
Ripe Literary Journal: "Penultimate"
Rockvale Review: "Exit, Stage Left"
Round Table Review: "Foster Child" and "New"
The Royal Vagrant Review: "Small Comforts"
Sheila-na-gig: "You Already Know"
Shō Poetry Journal: "The End of June," "Cleaning," "Something New," "Error," and "Odd People with Little Dogs"
Slipstream: "4th of July, 2008"
Snail Mail Review: "The Gentleman"
Spleen: "Siempre"
Sulphur River Literary Review: "Beware the Madman"
Thinking Out Loud: "The Photograph of Leopold Socha"
Third Wednesday Magazine: "10"
The Web: "4-21-93"
Trajectory: "When You're Old (VII)" and "When You're Old (VIII)"
Trailer Park Quarterly: "Trailer Park, Valdosta, Georgia, 1983"
Welter: "Personals"
White Pelican Review: "Safe"
Work to a Calm: "Recovery" and "Reminder"

ABOUT THE AUTHOR

Mike Buford

The poetry and prose of Robert L. Penick have appeared in nearly 200 different literary journals, including *The Hudson Review*, *North American Review*, *Plainsongs*, and *Oxford Magazine*. He has been chronicling the world and our interactions for more than forty years, from the vantage point of jailhouses, coffeehouses, and taverns, looking for humanity in every shard of glass and rusted bottle cap. Find more of his work at theartofmercy.net.

The Beggar Poet Series

The Beggar Poet Series is produced in partnership with *Shō Poetry Journal*, an imprint of Hohm Press, and is named for seekers across world traditions who set out on the spiritual path with nothing but a begging bowl in hand and a driving thirst for the unnameable. Some of those beggars become poets. Just as some poets, in their sacred vocation, become beggars, standing empty before the muse and writing what is given.

The Art of Mercy: New and Selected Poems is the first book in the Beggar Poet Series.

For more information, visit shopoetryjournal.com.